KidCaps' Presents
America in World War Two:
A History Just for Kids

KidCaps is An Imprint of BookCaps™
www.bookcaps.com

Table of Contents

About KidCaps

KidCaps is an imprint of BookCaps™ that is just for kids! Each month BookCaps will be releasing several books in this exciting imprint. Visit are website or like us on Facebook to see more!

American troops landed on Normandy Beach in France on
Tuesday, June 6, 1944.[1]

---

[1] Image source:
http://en.wikipedia.org/wiki/File:Into_the_Jaws_of_Death_23-
0455M_edit.jpg

4

Introduction

Robert Jones was terrified. He felt all sorts of strange feelings moving through his brain and rippling across his body. He felt seasick as the little boat bounced up and down over the waves, moving ever closer to the beach and to all the smoke. His hands gripped his rifle and were numb from a combination of the chill of the early morning air and the cold metal. His stomach tightened in knots as he thought about what was about to happen to him and to the soldiers around him. His platoon of about 30 soldiers was part of the United States' Army First Infantry Division, 16th Infantry Regiment, and their little amphibious troop carrier had just been launched out of a landing ship towards Omaha Beach, near the city of Normandy, in France.

Robert looked at the men around him and saw that most of them looked like they felt the way he did. Although Robert was the only one from the town of Topeka, most of the men in his platoon were from his home state of Kansas. None of them were used to travelling on the water, especially not on the way to fight in a war. One man threw up on the floor of the little boat, but no one said anything or made fun of him. They were all scared. The high walls of the boat didn't let them see what was going on around them, and they weren't too sure how much longer they had to wait. There were four men operating the boat, and those guys were too busy avoiding the obstacles put up by the German Army to talk to the soldiers.

Robert had heard the planes flying overhead during the night and knew that they were supposed to be bombing the beachhead before he and the other soldiers arrived. He had also heard about some sort of a plan by the men in charge to fool the Germans into thinking that the attack would be in a different part of France. But Robert was just a private in the army, so he didn't actually know how any of those plans were going, and he certainly didn't have the right to ask anyone about them. All he could hope for was that there would be fewer bullets flying at him when he got off of the landing craft and onto the beach.

The pilot of the landing craft, who was called the coxswain, yelled out some orders to the other crew members. Robert and the rest of the soldiers couldn't hear exactly what they said, but they soon understood the meaning as they felt the boat stop moving forward towards the shoreline.

They had arrived at Omaha Beach.

The gigantic metal ramp at the front of the landing craft was lowered down by one of the crewman, and the soldiers went charging out into the shallow water near the beach. They were met with a scene of utter chaos. The man right in front of Robert, Harry Jenkins, from Auburn, was shot through the head before they even made it off the boat. Robert didn't have time to think about it or to be sad because the Platoon Leader was yelling at all of the men to run out onto the beach and to try to find some cover. Robert put his head down and ran forward with the rest of his platoon.

His boots sunk into the wet sand and the sand and water seemed to explode all around him. He was too scared to lift up his head to look around because he knew that his helmet was the only thing protecting him. All Robert could think about was getting to the pile of rocks that he saw in front of him. As he ran forward, he tripped on a dead body lying on the beach- it was his Platoon Leader, Jeff Baker, from Colorado. Robert ran forward and dove onto the ground, hiding behind the rocks.

To his right and to his left, he could see that about 25 men from his platoon had made it. In the shallow water and on the sand, he could count six dead bodies. The water was already turning red with the blood. Further down the beach, he saw dozens of landing crafts like that one he had come in on lowering their ramps, and wave after wave of soldiers came spilling out onto the beach. His craft had already pulled itself back into the water and was heading back to the supply ship, the USS *Samuel Chase*, to bring more men to the beach.

—

6

His Platoon Sergeant had taken command of the group. Robert heard his name being yelled, and he snapped to attention. "Yes sir!" he yelled. The Sergeant explained that they were to take out the machine guns on the hill above them; otherwise no new troops would be able to make it to the beach. It would be difficult, and they would have to be smart, but the Sergeant knew that his men were up to the challenge. He asked the platoon if anyone had any grenades, and Robert showed the three that were clipped to his belt.

The Sergeant asked him. "Robert, how's your arm?"

With a nervous smile, Robert yelled over the sounds of the guns and the explosions: "Sir, I once pitched a no-hitter in high school."

The Sergeant yelled back: "Do you think you can get that grenade close enough to those guns to make them stop shooting for a few seconds, enough time for us move out from these rocks to the base of that hill?"

Robert lifted his head above the rocks for a moment to look at the distance, and almost immediately a hail of bullets splashed against the rocks around him. Ducking back down he said: "Yes, sir."

The Sergeant gave the order, Robert pulled the pin, threw the grenade, and the platoon rushed out towards the hill. Robert had arrived in Europe with the other Allied forces to fight in World War Two. He was among the first Americans to arrive, but more would follow after him. Many more.

Over 160,000 soldiers, including 73,000 Americans, landed in Normandy on June 6, 1944.[2]

Can you imagine riding in the landing craft next to Robert and the other soldiers? Can you imagine storming out onto Omaha Beach to fight against the German Nazis? Can you imagine how scary and difficult it would have been? The men and women who fought in World War Two had to experience some terrible and terrifying things. They saw their friends die, they went to foreign lands to fight against awful enemies, and each morning when they woke up, they never knew if that would be their last day alive.

World War Two was finally won by the Allied forces, and Americans were proud fight alongside the Allies. But what was World War Two all about, and how did Americans get involved in it? This handbook is going to teach us all about this war and the role that Americans helped play in it.

First, we will look at what led up to the outbreak of World War Two. For example, do you know what event marked the start of the War, and what conditions made it possible? Do you know

---

[2] Image source: http://www.army.mil/d-day/slideshow.html

---

why the United States waited so long to get involved? We will find out in this section.

Then, we will learn about the event that made the United State formally enter the War and what some of the first things that they did were. After that, we will see how the United States fought in World War Two on two separate fronts: in the European Theater and in the Pacific Theater. We will see some of the challenges that American soldiers had to deal with and some of the things that they saw and experience. World War Two also saw new types of technology being used and new strategies employed on the battlefield.

The next section will talk about what it was like to be a kid back then. Although no kids were allowed to fight in World War Two on either side, they were affected by what was going on. Things at home changed, and even school and meals were affected. We will see what it was like to be a kid both in America and in Europe.

The following section will talk about something more positive: the end of World War Two. We will see what events finally led to the end of this global conflict, both in Europe and then in the Pacific. Finally, we will see what happened after the war ended, including both the short-term and long-term consequences of the war.

War is a terrible thing, of that we can be sure. People die, it is scary, and lots of damage is done to innocent people and cities. Families are broken up, and entire nations disappear from the map. Yet, as awful as war is, sometimes it is necessary. As we will see, the world was facing several threats by leaders who wanted to hurt others and to take over entire continents. They would not take no for an answer, and one of them even went so far as to try to kill an entire race of people. Men like that have to be stopped, and sometimes war is the only way to do it.

But why should you care about a war that happened over 70 years ago? While many of the people who lived during that war and who fought in it have since died, we are still living in the world that World War Two helped to create. And sometimes, there are lots of scary men out there who need to be stopped, so war continues to be a reality. While we hope to never see anything like World War Two ever again, there are lots of valuable lessons that we can learn.

Are you ready to learn more about this important period of world history? Then let's begin with the first section.

Chapter 1: What Led Up to World War Two?

When you think of the causes of World War Two, you probably think of one person:

Adolf Hitler was the Chancellor of Germany during World War Two.[3]

While it is true that Adolf Hitler was one of the main aggressors during the war, he certainly could never have done all that he did were it not for certain political and economic conditions that existed at the time, and were it not for the similar political goals of Japan and Italy. The causes of World War Two are a little complex, but's let's take a minute to look at them, because then we will understand why so many people were willing to fight and die in this conflict.

Let's first look at what happened in Europe, shortly after World War One concluded. Do you remember who the principal

[3] Image   source:
http://en.wikipedia.org/wiki/File:Bundesarchiv_Bild_183-S33882,_Adolf_Hitler_retouched.jpg

aggressor was in that war? That's right: it was Germany! Germany had teamed up with Austria-Hungary to conquer all of Europe, including the neutral countries like Belgium. At the end of the war, after Germany had been forced to retreat after losing several pivotal battles, the Treaty of Versailles was signed to put an official end to the hostilities. Along with making peace, the Treaty of Versailles made Germany suffer a lot of consequences for having done so much damage during the war. Among other things, Germany agreed to pay "reparations" to the Allied powers in the equivalent of about US$442 billion today. But where did all of that money come from? The money had to come from the German economy, of course.

The Treaty of Versailles made it clear that the payments had to be made in gold or foreign currency- considered much more stable by the other countries. So in order to pay the debts, Germany had to convert its money into foreign currency in order to buy gold in order to pay the reparations. Got it? But as they kept buying more and more foreign currency and foreign gold, the value of the German currency went down, meaning that they needed more money to buy even basic items, like loaves of bread and bottles of milk. Soon, even basic items were almost impossible for the Germany people to obtain.

The difficult economic situation was bad enough, but there was also the German pride. In the Treaty of Versailles, note Article 231:

> "The Allied and Associated Governments affirm and Germany accepts the responsibility of Germany and her allies for causing all the loss and damage to which the Allied and Associated Governments and their nationals have been subjected as a consequence of the war imposed upon them by the aggression of Germany and her allies."

This article makes it clear that Germany (along with its allies) caused all the problems from World War One. Many of the German people felt insulted by this and thought that the whole world was laughing at Germany. This led to a feeling called

---

12

"nationalism", where the people wanted to see their country receive the respect and attention that they thought it deserved. It was during this time; a time when the people were looking for a new type of government to fix the economic problems and to make Germany glorious again, that Adolf Hitler and his National Socialist political party came to power and Hitler started to carry out his dark plans for the country.

In the meantime, Italy had political ambitions of its own. Once home to the impressive and powerful Roman Empire, the country had since begun to experience economic problems and was no longer dominating the Mediterranean Sea as it once did. As Germany began to shift towards nationalistic goals (meaning goals that made people feel good about Germany) Italy saw a chance to take advantage of their strength and to make a formal agreement with them and announced it on November 1, 1936. This agreement would also help both sides to fight together against a new threat in Europe: Communism from Russia. Also, Italy hoped to once again become a powerful nation and to rule over the Mediterranean like before.

In the meantime, Japan had ambitions of its own. Because it desired to be the dominant country in Asia, it had begun to fight against China and even to invade Chinese lands and to kill innocent civilians. By 1937, the Empire of Japan and the Republic of China were already at war, and Japan was interested in finding someone to help them win their war, and to stop anyone who got in their way.

On September 27, 1940, Germany, Italy, and Japan signed a momentous agreement called the Tripartite Pact, and these three nations became known as the Axis alliance. Although they never got quite organized to be able to send money and troops to help each other out, they were united by their common goals of expanding their territories. The way they saw it, these three countries were going to be the dominant powers in Europe and Asia. Also, they all agreed that they hated Russian Communism and would do anything to stop it.

So the economic circumstances and political ambitions of these three countries were the principal reason for the outbreak of World War Two. When these countries decided to start attacking and mistreating their neighbors, the other countries of the world saw that the aggressors had to be stopped. Most historians feel that the official start to World War Two was on September 1, 1939, when Hitler's German Army invaded its innocent neighbor, Poland.

You may be asking yourself: where was the United States during all of this? Do you remember how the United States had fought in World War One? A lot of the people who were alive just twenty years later, when Hitler invaded Germany, had unusually unpleasant memories of fighting in Europe. They remembered how badly America had suffered along with the rest of the world and how so many American soldiers had died. Also, the country had just experienced a rough economic time called the Great Depression, so a lot of people were worried about making a terrible situation even worse.

In order to make sure that the United States didn't get involved in any more wars, Congress passed a series of laws called the Neutrality Acts. Three acts, passed between 1935 and 1937, made it impossible for the United States to trade weapons of supplies with nations who were at war (whether they were the good guys or the bad guys) and even prevented passengers from travelling on ships of nations at war. The goal was to keep the American people as far away as possible from the conflicts of other nations. President Franklin D. Roosevelt, President of the U.S. at the time, had even said: "I have said this before, but I shall say it again and again: your boys are not going to be sent into any foreign wars."[4]

What do you think? Was that the best way for the American people to handle the situation? What would you have done if you had been the president?

---

[4] Quotation source: http://www.history.co.uk/explore-history/ww2/us-entry-and-alliance.html

Although he didn't want to get involved in other people's fights, President Roosevelt was still worried that the acts might end up helping the bad guys, like Germany. How so? If the U.S. were to stand by and not help England and France, then it could be like making the war easier for Germany, something that everyone agreed was a lousy idea. Finally, after Germany attacked Poland in 1939, the previous Neutrality Acts were repealed, and the United States was allowed to help out the Allied forces on a limited basis. In March of 1941, a new Act, called the Lend-Lease Act, ended American neutrality and allowed the U.S. to sell, lend, or even give weapons and other support to any nation that the government wanted to, even if that nation was at war.

Most Americans, including those in the government, had wanted to remain neutral. What changed their opinion? As was the case with World War One, the Americans began to hear about the terrible things happening in Europe, and they realized that a Europe dominated by extremists like Hitler and Mussolini (the dictator in Italy) would be ruinous for everyone.

United States ships began to escort other ships that were carrying supplies for the Allies, and some of these ships were sunk by German U-Boats (submarines) something that made many Americans angry and helped them to realize that the war was getting closer and closer to home.

The American people began to prepare for war, especially after France was defeated in 1940 and Italy allied itself with Germany. People began to ration food in order to give more supplies to the growing army. A peacetime draft was put into effect, the first in the nation's history, forcing American men to join the armed forces, although there were already lots of volunteers. Also, for the first time ever, women were allowed to play a larger role in the military. Some 110,000 women joined the Women's Army Auxiliary Corps (WAAC) and served both in the U.S. and overseas, in non-combat positions, allowing more men to go to the front and fight. Also, women began to serve in non-combat position in the Air Force, in an organization called the Women Air force Service Pilots (WASP), whose job was to help train anti-aircraft gunners by towing targets and to carry cargo from one place to another.

The United States was no longer neutral and was preparing for a fight that everyone knew was coming. However, they were still determined not to enter the fight unless they were forced to. What kind of an event could force the American people to support entry into World War Two- the most destructive of all wars in history? Let's find out.

Chapter 2: Why did the United States enter into World War Two?

As we have seen, the United States did not want to get involved in another country's war. But the American people as a whole would be willing to fight in a war if it meant protecting themselves and their interests. On December 7, 1941, the war that was raging around the world was brought to the American doorstep. What happened?

The Japanese had already made it clear that they wanted to dominate the continent of Asia and that they didn't want any interference by the United States or other Allied countries. In order to make sure that the U.S. and other countries would be unable to stop them, the Japanese Navy launched a preemptive strike on several different targets, including Pearl Harbor, in Hawaii. A "preemptive" strike is an attack that comes as a surprise, with no warning. Below, you can see a picture taken by a Japanese plane of that attack:

A torpedo causes an explosion on the *USS Oklahoma*.[5]

The goal was to destroy as much of the U.S. Navy in the Pacific as possible so that it would not be able to stop the nation of Japan from conquering Asia. Several other attacks in Thailand and Hong Kong, carried out at almost the same moment, also were aimed at stopping the Americans and other Allied countries from being able to fight back.

The attack at Pearl Harbor was truly devastating. Because the attack was totally unexpected, and because it came very early in the morning, many of the men were still sleeping and were not ready to fight. The planes were out in the open (to guard against sabotage) but that made them easy targets for the attackers. The Japanese planes came in two waves, dropping heavy bombs, torpedoes, and shooting machine gun fire. Submarines also took part, and historians think that one "midget" submarine (a small submarine launched by a larger boat that only carried two crew members) was able to sink the *USS Virginia*.

In total, the attack against Pearl Harbor and some local airfields lasted about ninety minutes, but the damage was particularly extensive. All eight U.S. Navy battleships that were stationed at Pearl Harbor were damaged, and four of them were sunk. Later, two of them were raised, and the other four were repaired so that eventually six of the eight went out to battle in the war. The Japanese planes also sank or damaged other smaller ships: three cruisers, three destroyers, an anti-aircraft training ship, and one minelayer. There were also other damages: 188 U.S. aircraft were destroyed during the attack, 2,402 Americans were killed and another 1,282 were wounded.

The *USS Arizona* was sunk after it was hit by a Japanese bomb.[6]

The attack was devastating, and the American people realized that they could no longer be neutral in the war. They realized that the war was about defending themselves as well as stopping the bad guys who wanted to hurt others. The next day, on

[6] Image source: http://aboutjapan.japansociety.org/content.cfm/uss_arizona

December 8, 1941, President Roosevelt went before Congress and delivered a speech in which he spoke about how awful it was what the Japanese had done, and how the American people had to react. He outlined how dangerous the nation of Japan was acting and in his speech he said:

> "Yesterday, December 7th, 1941 -- a date which will live in infamy -- the United States of America was suddenly and deliberately attacked by naval and air forces of the Empire of Japan... The attack yesterday on the Hawaiian Islands has caused severe damage to American naval and military forces. I regret to tell you that very many American lives have been lost. In addition, American ships have been reported torpedoed on the high seas between San Francisco and Honolulu. Yesterday, the Japanese government also launched an attack against Malaya. Last night, Japanese forces attacked Hong Kong. Last night, Japanese forces attacked Guam. Last night, Japanese forces attacked the Philippine Islands. Last night, the Japanese attacked Wake Island. And this morning, the Japanese attacked Midway Island.
> Japan has, therefore, undertaken a surprise offensive extending throughout the Pacific area. The facts of yesterday and today speak for themselves. The people of the United States have already formed their opinions and well understand the implications to the very life and safety of our nation...I ask that the Congress declare that since the unprovoked and dastardly attack by Japan on Sunday, December 7th, 1941, a state of war has existed between the United States and the Japanese empire."

Congress approved the vote, and the United States officially declared war against the Empire of Japan. Four days later, Germany, an ally of Japan, declared war on the United States.

The United States had officially entered World War Two, and had the unique challenge of fighting a war on two fronts: one in Europe (against Germany and Italy) and one in the Pacific (against Japan). What did the Americans and the Allied forces do to win the war? Let's find out.

Chapter 3: What Happened During World War Two?

Once the United States had decided to join World War Two, there was no time to be lost. They had desperate enemies to fight against, and these evil people needed to be stopped.

The first priority was to halt the nearly unstoppable movement of Japan in the Pacific. The United States fought back, and the first battle was fought from May 4-8, 1942 at the Coral Sea near Australia. This war was intriguing because the enemy ships never actually saw each other. Using the new technology of radar and large aircraft carriers, they simply sent planes back and forth to attack each other's ships. Although the Japanese were able to seriously hurt the Allied forces, even killing 656 sailors and pilots, they themselves were stopped for the first time in their military campaign. The Japanese also suffered heavy losses, including 966 people killed and five ships sunk. During the next major sea battle between the Americans and the Japanese, the missing men and ships made it a more of an equal battle.

The Battle of Midway was fought from June 4-7, 1942 and was a definite American victory. The Japanese had hoped to lure the Americans into a trap and to take over the island of Midway to use as a base during the war. However, the Americans were able to intercept and decipher the coded transmissions and to figure out where the next attack would be. They were ready when the Japanese arrived, and the battle was intense. In just four short days, the Japanese lost four carriers and one cruiser, with a total of 3,057 persons killed. The Americans only lost one carrier and one destroyer, with 307 people dead.

From that moment on, the Americans were no longer defending themselves; they began to go on the offensive, pushing the Japanese fleet further and further back towards Japan.

In the meantime, American forces began to arrive and fight in Europe. On November 8, 1942, Operation Torch was carried out using American and Allied soldiers in North Africa.

American troops arrived on the beaches of North Africa on November 8, 1942.[7]

The goal was to get rid of Axis soldiers in North Africa in order to gain control of the Mediterranean and to be able to invade Europe from the south, forcing Hitler to fight on two fronts (one with Russia in the north, one with the Allies in the south). The initial battle lasted about eight days, and the Allies won. The Americans had contributed to this first historic victory in the war against the Axis powers!

The Allies spent the next year fighting against Italian forces, who finally surrendered on June 4, 1944. However, the biggest contribution of the Americans to the Allied war effort took place two days later, on June 6, 1944, at an event that came to be known as "D-Day". Part of Operation Overload, on this day tens of thousands of Allied troops landed on the beaches of Normandy, France, in order to open up a massive second front in the war with Germany. As we saw in the introduction, it was a terrible struggle, and some 6,000 Americans died on the beaches

---

[7]   Image   source: http://en.wikipedia.org/wiki/File:Torch-troops_hit_the_beaches.jpg

that day, but their courage and bravery allowed the Allies to get a foothold in Europe and to start moving troops and supplies to fight the war there.

The soldiers then spent the next few months slowly moving inland, fighting against the German forces. Paris was liberated from Nazi control on August 25, and the Allies kept pushing the Germans further and further back towards where they came from. On December 16, the Germans tried to push back against the advancing allies and to break their lines. In this huge battle, called the Battle of the Bulge, there were eventually some 610,000 Allied soldiers, mainly American, fighting against a large German army of about 250,000 soldiers. The fighting was fierce, but by the end of the four-week battle, the Germans had lost. Some 100,000 German soldiers had died or had been wounded, compared to 89,000 American troops.

The Battle of the Bulge (named for the shape in the Allied battle lines when the Germans attacked and made them retreat) was an important turning point for many reasons. Not only did it show how dedicated the Americans were to defeating Hitler, but it also allowed African-Americans to fight on the front lines for the first time. This battle also drained Germany's reserve forces to the limit. Germany had bet everything on beating the Allies, and they had lost. It was the beginning of the end for Germany.

Meanwhile, in the Pacific, the war against the Japanese was going more and more in favor of the Allies. After winning the Battle of Midway, the Allies began to push the Japanese back towards their homeland. Instead of wasting lots of time conquering each and every one of the thousands of islands in the Pacific, it was decided that the Allies would have a campaign of "island-hopping" where they would move from one island to another, skipping the small ones, to get closer and closer to the Japanese mainland.

The United States had entered World War Two on December 8, 1942. By early 1945, they had helped to stop the Axis forces on both fronts and were pushing them back where they had come from. They were finally winning the war.

Chapter 4: What Was it Like to be a Kid During World War Two?

As we saw in the introduction, kids were not allowed to fight in the war as part of any army. However, like the rest of the world, kids knew what was going on and they were affected by it. Let's talk first about what it was like to be a kid in the U.S., and then we will talk about some of the sad stuff that kids in Europe saw.

Kids living in the United States during World War Two saw their lives get turned upside down. First off, they found that it got harder and harder to buy the food and clothing that they were used to having. Why? As raw materials (the things we use to make stuff) started to be used more and more to help the soldiers of Allied nations, there was less for the people at home. What was the solution? Ration books.

A ration book determined how much food a family could buy at the store.[8]

A ration book was assigned to each person in the family, even to the babies. It made sure that everybody could get a little bit of something (although they often wanted more). The first things to be rationed were car tires (for the rubber), but soon all kinds of things had to be rationed: coffee, sugar, meat, cheese, gasoline, butter, canned, foods, and even bicycles. Some new items (like cars and appliances) weren't even made during the war. All of the materials needed to be used to make bullets and airplanes and other things to help the soldiers fighting in the war.

As a kid living in the U.S., you would have had to eat your favorite foods less often. A lot of families decided to grow food at home, and called their gardens "Victory Gardens" or "War Gardens" because of the way they contributed to the war effort. Your mom might have asked you to go out and dig in the

---

[8]   Image   source:
http://allthenutsinthetree.blogspot.com/2011_04_01_archive.html

garden, and from time to time you may have gotten to help to pick fresh vegetables and spices.

Although there weren't too many attacks on American soil, everyone was constantly aware of the threat from both the Japanese and German armies. However, did you know that both the Japanese and Germany militaries tried to attack the United States mainland? It's true! And some kids were pretty scared when it happened.

The Japanese tried to send "balloon bombs" to the American mainland. They sewed together gargantuan balloons and filled them with hydrogen air. Then, they attached bombs to these balloons and let them go up into the Jetstream, a current of wind that goes from Japan to North America. Over 3,000 of these balloons were launched, but just a few made it to the United States, and only one claimed any victims. But can you imagine what it was like for many American kids to be afraid of a balloon bomb dropping down on them from the sky?

On the other side of the country, long range German submarines had been able to travel as all the way to New York harbor. At night, they would look out their periscopes and look for the outline of ships against the city lights. They sunk so many ships that eventually the government had to ask people to turn off their lights at night so that the submarines couldn't see the silhouettes of the boats anymore in order to sink them. Kids had to practice turning out the lights whenever the government told them to.

Also, in the United States, many kids had to spend less time with their moms. Why? Well, because many moms went to work in large factories where materials for the wars were made, like you can see in the picture below.

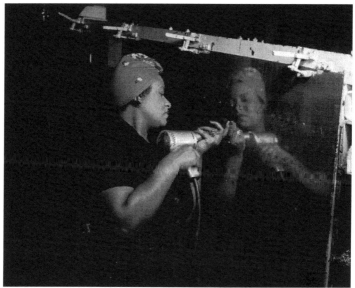

A hard-working factory worker puts in the rivets on part of a dive bomber.[9]

Kids in the United States had to think a lot about the war and wonder when their dads and brothers were coming home, or even *if* they were coming home. However, for kids in Europe (and some parts of Asia), they didn't just think about the war; they lived it every day.

Think about what it meant for kids who lived in a war zone. Many times, they had to evacuate cities as armies moved in. Sometimes their houses were destroyed by bombs, their families were arrested and sent to prison, and sometimes they had to live with foster parents or relatives after the war was over. In Europe, some innocent kids had to see some terrible things. Like what? Do you remember what Adolf Hitler wanted to do? That's right: he wanted to conquer all of Europe and to stop Communism from spreading. However, he also wanted to get rid of certain

[9] Image source: http://en.wikipedia.org/wiki/File:Rosie_the_Riveter_(Vultee)_DS.jpg

people that he saw as "undesirable", or not as good as others. Among them were Jewish people, Gypsies, handicapped people, and even certain religions like Jehovah's Witnesses, who refused to go along with what Hitler wanted. What did Hitler do with all these people?

He would round them up and take them to "work camps". At these camps, some people were forced to make clothing and weapons for the German army while others were simply executed. Even children were taken to these camps and mistreated, and sometimes they were even killed.

It's not pleasant to think about such sad things happening. It's even hard to think how the German guards and soldiers went along with Hitler. Some were too scared to say no; others actually agreed with him. What do you think: was it right of Hitler to round up people based on their background or religious beliefs and ship them by train to far away prisons, only to kill them? Of course not. Some six million people, mostly of Jewish descent, died in these camps. This period of time came to be known as The Holocaust, and we should never forget that it happened so that we can prevent something like it from happening again.

Hitler took prisoners of war and even fellow Germans to concentration camps like this one, called Auschwitz.[10]

Being a kid during World War Two was difficult in the United States, and it was an absolute nightmare in Europe.

---

[10] Image source: http://wp.lehman.edu/lehman-today/2012/04/lehman-professor-leads-holocaust-educators-on-visit-to-historical-sites-in-poland-and-israel/

Chapter 5: How Did World War Two End?

As we saw earlier, World War Two was being fought against two main enemies: Germany and Japan (Italy had already surrendered earlier to the Allied forces). We know that the Allies eventually won, but how did the bad guys actually lose? Let's find out.

First, let's look at Germany. As we saw, the Battle of the Bulge was a huge defeat for the German army. They had some 100,000 casualties, and they had not gained any of their objectives. The Soviets (Russians) were pushing harder and harder on the eastern flank, and Germany was soon retreating in Italy also. All of the large gains that Germany had made during the war were being lost, one step at a time, as the troops were forced to retreat over and over and over again.

On February 4, 1945, the leaders of the Allies met with Soviet leader Joseph Stalin in Ukraine to discuss what should happen to Germany after the war. It was clear that Germany was close to being stopped.

Winston Churchill, Franklin D. Roosevelt, and Joseph Stalin met together to discuss the war.[11]

It was discussed that the Soviet Union would enter the war against Japan at a future date and that Germany would be occupied by the allies after the war.

On April 30, 1945, Allied forces captured the Reichstag (the German capital building) and Adolf Hitler (hidden in a secret bunker in the same city) committed suicide by swallowing poison. Germany had been defeated, and on May 8, Germany officially signed a document of surrender. The day was declared Victory in Europe day. But the war wasn't over yet.

Let's have a look at Japan. As you may remember, the Pacific Theater had a lot of genuinely tough fighting. Huge ships used planes and large guns to attack each other, and the Allies (including the United States at The Battle of Midway) were finally able to stop the offensive of the Japanese navy and to start to push them back towards Asia.

[11] Image source: http://en.wikipedia.org/wiki/Yalta_Conference

Once they arrived at the thousands of islands that surround Japan, the Allies decided to focus on the larger ones (the islands with room for airports and military bases) that they could use to prepare for the next stage of getting closer and closer to Japan.

In January 1945, the Allies had made it to the Philippines, and by May they were in Borneo. The Allies were imagining that there would be another long war like there had been in Europe, with soldiers moving bit by bit towards the capital, fighting every step of the way. Russia made plans to invade from the north, and the Allies planned to move in from the south. However, before a full-scale invasion was started, the Allies wanted to weaken the Japanese fighting force. They did this by means of a weapon that had worked well in Europe- firebombing.

Do you know what firebombing is? A normal bomb, when dropped on a city, uses a large explosion to destroy buildings and to kill people. However, a firebomb has a smaller explosion, but its main goal is to start lots of little fires that spread across a city. The Allies wanted to burn down military bases and factories so that the Japanese would not be able to fight as well when the invasion came. Most of the large cities in Japan were firebombed, and it is estimated that hundreds of thousands of people were killed. For example, in February of 1945, some 100,000 people in Tokyo alone died as a result of firebombing. It was a scary time.

The Empire of Japan was still fighting and would not surrender. Before launch the invasion that they had planned, the United States decided to use a brand new bomb that they had been secretly developing. It was called the Atomic Bomb. The Atomic Bomb used a new type of technology to create larger and deadlier explosions and shockwaves, and the covered the area with radiation afterwards.

34

The two atomic bombs dropped in Japan made immense mushroom clouds.[12]

The United States was sure that dropping these incredibly damaging bombs would help convince Japan to surrender quickly. They knew that the destructive would scare a lot of people and that the psychological (emotional) effect would be even more effective than the destruction. The target cities were based on size and usefulness. Eventually, two bombs were dropped in 1945, on the cities of Hiroshima (August 6) and Nagasaki (on August 9). The Allies wanted unconditional surrender from Japan, and they finally received it on August 15.

World War Two had been fought and won by the Allies. The violence and pain were finally over.

---

[12] Image source: http://en.wikipedia.org/wiki/File:Atomic_bombing_of_Japan.jpg

Chapter 6: What Happened After World War Two?

Once the fighting had stopped, the world needed to start to heal. Cities needed to be rebuilt, the dead needed to be buried, and the world needed to make sure that Germany would not be a threat again. The first main problem was what to do with Germany.

The Allies decided that Germany would have to be occupied for some time by foreign troops until a stable, friendly government could be established. It was decided that the Soviet Union would occupy the eastern part of Germany and the rest of the allies the western part. In time, two remarkably different Germany's emerged: a democratic Germany in the west and a communist Germany in the east. This strange creation, a country split into two parts, would last throughout the next forty-plus years.

In order to prevent something as terrible as World War Two (and the Holocaust) from ever happening again, the Allied forces held trials to prosecute and execute the leadership of Nazi Germany. Although Adolf Hitler and a few other high-ranking officials had committed suicide, others were taken to trial, sentenced, and executed for the horrible things that they had done.

In Asia, Japan had agreed to a total surrender, so the lands that they had conquered were given back to the original owners. China, now no longer worrying about war with Japan, experienced a civil war and became a communist nation. The country of Korea found itself in a position remarkably similar to that of Germany- it was divided into two parts, and one (the northern part) became communist and the other (the southern part) democratic. The tensions became strong, and an awful war would erupt in that tiny peninsula in 1950.

Although the League of Nations, an international group of ambassadors meant to prevent world war, had failed to prevent World War Two, many people still felt optimistic that the countries of the world could solve their problems without war if they just had a place to get together and talk things out. As a result, on October 24, 1945, the United Nations was formed in order to prevent a third world war from breaking out, and so far it has been successful.

World War Two left a total of some 60 million people dead. Can you even imagine such a large number? At the time, it was about two out of every one hundred people dying. It would be as if the entire population of the United Kingdom disappeared, or if everyone in the states of California and New York suddenly died. After so much death, the world needed time to heal.

However, the construction of the atomic bomb made a lot of governments realize how fast a war could be fought. They realized how many people could be killed in a matter of minutes. The next few decades saw the Unites States and the USSR (Russia) start to race to build stronger and better bombs, just in case a war broke out. The Cold War, as it was called, would last until the early 1990s.

Conclusion

This has been a truly fascinating handbook because it's let us learn about one of the most pivotal times in human history- a time when almost the entire world was at war with each other. A lot of terrible things happened, and a lot of people died. However, some seriously bad people were stopped, and a lot of lives were saved.

Do you remember all of the interesting things that we learned? Let's review. First, we looked at what led up to the outbreak of World War Two. We saw how three separate nations, Italy, Germany, and Japan, all got together in order see how they could make their countries larger and more powerful. Although Japan had invaded China a few years earlier, most historians feel that World War Two actually started with Adolf Hitler's invasion of Poland in 1939. The United States tried to stay neutral at first, and then they tried to just give money and weapons to the Allied forces.

Then, we learned about the event that made the United States formally enter the war. Do you remember what that event was? It was the bombing of Pearl Harbor on December 7, 1941. The Japanese had wanted to make sure that the Americans wouldn't get in their way as they tried to take over Asia, so they launched a massive attack against the American naval ships stationed at Pearl Harbor, in Hawaii. A lot of people died, but the Navy was able to repair many of the ships and get back out into the ocean to fight against the Japanese. Their first job was to get the ships up and running again to stop Japan, and then to get troops over to Europe to fight against Italy and Germany.

After that, we saw how the United States fought in World War Two on two separate fronts: in the European Theater and in the Pacific Theater. The Pacific Theater was all about naval warfare, and the world got to see massive groups of ships sending planes back and forth to sink each other. After the historic Battle of Midway, the United States gained the upper hand and began to push the Japanese back towards their home island. From there, the battle changed to "island hopping", moving closer and closer to the mainland.

In Europe, after landing in Africa and pushing north into Europe, the Allies helped to defeat Italy and start pushing the Germany army northwards. Meanwhile, with the massive invasion of troops on D-Day, a second front was created (in addition to the one with Russia) and Hitler had to fight a two-front war. After a series of victories, culminating in the Battle of the Bulge, Hitler's armies started a long retreat back to Berlin, the capital of Germany. The war was starting to go in favor of the Allies.

The next section talked about what it was like to be a kid back then. Although no kids were allowed to fight in World War Two on either side, they were affected by what was going on. Things at home changed, and even school and meals were affected. We also saw how kids had to practice blackouts (to help ships avoid getting sunk by submarines) and had to ration their food. We also learned about some of the terrible things that kids in Europe saw like the people killed by the Holocaust. It was a sad time.

The following section talked about something more positive: the end of World War Two. We saw what events finally led to the end of this global conflict, both in Europe and then in the Pacific. Do you remember what they were? In Europe, the Battle of the Bulge was the last time that the German army tried to push back the advancing Allies and to break their battle lines. Although they came close, the large number of fresh American troops was finally too much, and the Germans had to retreat. Soon, Hitler committed suicide, and the Germans surrendered.

In the Pacific, we learned how effective the island hopping campaign was. It allowed the Allied forces to get remarkably close to the Japanese mainland. Bombers weakened the large cities, and finally two atomic bombs were dropped. After seeing the destructive new weapons, the Japanese surrendered unconditionally. The war had finally ended.

Finally, we saw what happened after the war ended, including both the short-term and long-term consequences of the war. Some of the short term consequences had to do with rebuilding Europe and Asia and helping to punish the people that had caused so much trouble. Some of the long-term consequences involved forming a dual-power Germany and Korea, both of which became supremely important issues during the Cold War that followed.

World War Two was a time when the entire world was at war, and their governments, industries, and citizens all got together to support the war effort. Over 60 million people died, and we should never forget their sacrifice. If you know someone who fought in or was affected by World War Two, why not ask them about it?

If you know a veteran of World War Two, why not ask them about their experience?[13]

---

[13] Image source: http://dav44.org/

72400837R00024

Made in the USA
San Bernardino, CA
24 March 2018